WHAT IS YOUR PRICE OF ADMISSION

DISCOVER who you are. *DECIDE* where you are going & *SET* goals to get there.

SHARON V. DICKEY

What Is Your Price of Admission?

Copyright © 2019 Vander Publishing House

The following is a work of inspiration, based on the author's life journey and true personal encounters, that is guided by her own personal relationship with God. No real names are used to protect the identity of those she has loved.

For information contact:

Sharon V. Dickey, LPCA, NCC
My Reason Why Counseling Services
https://www.sharondickey.com

ISBN: 978-0-578-47577-6 (paperback)
Cover Illustration by Sharon V. Dickey Copyright © 2019
Edited By: Angie Writes 4 Me
(angiewrites4me@gmail.com)

All Rights Reserved. No part of this publication or any of its contents may be reproduced, copied, stored in a retrieval system, transmitted, modified or adapted in any form or by any means, electronic, mechanical, photocopying, recording or otherwise, except as permitted under section 107 or 108 or the 1976 United States Copyright Act, without the prior written consent of the author or publisher.

To,

all my family and friends, for encouraging me to be me.

To my Sister and Bestie for being my biggest cheerleaders, constantly pouring into me, believing in me, supporting me, questioning me, and correcting me.

To "My Reasons Why" for riding with me and unconditionally loving me through it all.

Table of Contents

Preface

Self-Awareness – conscious knowledge of one's own character, feelings, motives, and desires.

Chapter 1   The Purpose 1

Chapter 2   I Forgive Me 5

Chapter 3   I'm a Big Deal 13

Chapter 4   What is Your Price of Admission? 23

Self Esteem – confidence in one's own worth or abilities; self-respect.

Chapter 5   Fine as Hell, but Still Single as Ever ...29

Chapter 6   What is Your Worth? 35

Chapter 7   Pinky Toe 51

Chapter 8 How to Get Rid of a Man with No Intentions 71

Chapter 9 Stranger Danger! 77

Chapter 10 Ghosted Again? 85

Goals – The destination of a journey

Chapter 11 I'll Do Fine If I Just be Me 97

Chapter 12 What Do You Want From Me? 101

Chapter 13 Keep Dreaming and Believing............109

Chapter 14 No Worry, No Fear ....…........... 121

Preface

I was unfulfilled in every way you can possibly imagine in my last marriage. It was a rough 4 1/2 years, and after separating and moving to another state, I still fought for the marriage making accommodations to try and allow my ex-husband to be involved in our lives, but he just did not want that. There is no co-parenting, although I desperately wanted him to be more involved in his children's lives, God knew he was not the ideal person to have influence over our children, so I am thankful I have been able to be the sole parent with a lot of help from my parents.

The journey here was long, exhausting, and frustrating at times where all I wanted to do was lay down and cry. It baffled me to think about how someone had such a distaste for me that they would completely abandon their kids. He was never mean or rude towards me. I couldn't figure out if he hated me or liked me. It was just confusing as to what makes a person not want to wake up to their beautiful children every day, so in my mind, the problem had to be with me. He told me countless times, I didn't do anything wrong, but I continued to blame myself. After I had done all I could do, it came to me that I really was not the problem. He was a person that could not relate to me on any level. We could only talk politics because he watched CNN religiously, but even then, he wasn't able to think freely and have his own perspective on things. Everything that he had accomplished in his adult life was because I helped him in some way. I had taken care of him the entire time we were together, and I was still taking care of him after I separated from him. The day finally came where I had to face the reality that my children will not grow up with both of their parents in the same house as I did as a child. I had to acknowledge that my daughter would not have a Daddy's girl relationship with her own father, which was most heartbreaking for me. I had to accept the fact that I would be a single parent raising my children in a broken home. I had to accept the fact that I was going to be alone and would have to enter this ridiculous dating game all over again.

But God is so amazing! God has provided for us, and we have always had everything we needed. My favorite scripture is when God said "Let your conduct be without covetousness; be content with such things as you have. For He, Himself has said, "I will never leave you nor forsake you." Hebrews 13:5 NKJV. He has never left us. We have never gone without. As a matter of fact, the more I learned to lean on Him and His words, the better our lives got. My personal relationship with God grew, and my faith increased tremendously.

It took 4 years, after me and my children left Atlanta, to free myself of that marriage and file for divorce. It took me that long to conquer the fear of moving from that stage in my life to the next stage. I had no idea what God had in store for me. As soon as I left, it was like God had said: "It's about time." I've been waiting on you to move out of the way so I can do what I do". The day I got that divorce decree, I felt like I was given another chance to do things right this time. I hit the ground running, continually finding ways to improve myself. I remembered I had goals of the life I wanted for myself that got pushed to the side while I was dealing with that marriage. Finally, I was getting back to myself. I had overcome health issues. I was driving again. I bought a new car, and we moved out into our own apartment. I finally finished my master's degree, passed the state board test, and was awarded my counseling license.

With all the things I set out to accomplish, I pushed dating off to the sidelines. I gave it several tries, but dating in this millennium is nothing like it was in the '90s. I had to give that up and get clear about that aspect of my life as well. I decided to wait on God to send the one for me. We discussed the qualities I wanted this amazing man to have, and then God placed wise people around me, and he made sure I learned from my past mistakes to ensure my next husband would be God's choice and not my own. I don't make the decisions for my life. I sit back and wait for God to make those decisions because he has proven to me repeatedly that what He can provide for me is way better than anything I can ever try to get for myself.

I have come a long way, and now I am ready to start the next chapter of my life. This whole inspirational, motivational speaking, and counseling isn't new for me. I have been pouring into people for many years, and for many years, people have been encouraging me to continue to do so, but on a larger scale. I thought about my first book. "My Reason Why," was going to be all I had to do, but God quickly showed me in many ways that His expectations of me are far greater than my expectations for myself. I am finally to the point where I know exactly who I am. I know where I am going, and I know how I am going to get there. I have learned to live my authentic self every day, and not be ashamed of who God created me to be or allow others to mute the greatness in me. I have always been a little outside the box. I have never liked to follow straight lines, although I did so because that was what I thought I was supposed to do. Now, I understand I must get off that smooth cookie-cutter road and travel along an uncomfortable path to continue pushing myself forward and loving the uniqueness of me. I am Sharon V. Dickey, and I love being me!

"I don't mind patiently waiting for what God has for me."

Sharon V. Dickey

Chapter 1

The Purpose

The purpose of this book is to encourage you to find out who you are, decide what direction you want to go in life, and inspire you to set goals and actively work towards achieving them. Once you realize who you are, it makes understanding your purpose easier. When I speak of purpose, I am talking about discovering why you were even born. You will have to ask God to tell you what your purpose is in life. Your purpose will send you on a journey. You will have many ups as you climb high mountains and many downs as you fight your way through low valleys. The road you will take will never go straight east to west or north to south. It will change directions so many times that you may find yourself lost. That is when you learn the importance of the process. The process happens along the journey. There is a price to pay for everything you desire to have. You can have all of your desires, based on God's words, but you will have to work hard for them and have faith that God's plan for your life and his timing is not your own. You may have to wait and be patient while you are going through the process and believe that God is working in the background preparing everything to be perfect for you and that may take some time. The process is a very trying time, and things are very intense to where you may feel discouraged or even alone. It is essential to know that this is the stage where the devil expects you to give up and quit. To make it to the finish line, you have to dig deep within, stay committed to fulfilling your destiny, and trust that God has not left you hanging, he's just busy moving things around to clear the path ahead for you. You have to stay focused on your goals and keep working the plan so that you achieve your goals. Finding your purpose will inspire you to live your true self, and it will motivate you to dream again. Your dreams are visions of the life God wants you to live. Writing down your dreams and creating a workable plan is what you have to do to let go and take that first step and trust God to carry you to the end. Think of what it is like to set something on fire. Becoming inspired is like lighting a match; first, you have a "spark" of inspiration that creates fire. Fire is the "energy" of motivation. Then you take that fire and touch something to ignite it, but you have to decide what to touch. That is where you "envision" what you want and "set your goals." Now that you've decided what you want to light on fire, then you have to make a "plan of action" to get it done. So, seek inspiration, take that energy to motivate yourself into action by setting goals and creating a plan of action to achieve those goals.

God said He "will never leave you nor forsake you." He will be there with you every step of the way through finding your purpose, stepping out on your journey, going through the process, and reaching your destiny. God is able! He can, and He will give you everything your heart desire if you trust Him, believe in His promises, and have faith that He will be with you and guide you through. Let my words be a source of inspiration to you. I pray I can be the spark you need to start living the life of your dreams.

"Stop telling people you don't choose who you fall in love with. That dumb idea was all yours." Sharon V. Dickey

Chapter 2

I Forgive Me

We got a lot to cover and no time to waste! Let's start this book off by acknowledging our past. Hi, my name is Sharon Dickey, and I have a past. Guess what? We all have a past, and we all have things that we have gone through that have been wonderful and challenging in our past. Let's take a second and celebrate all the beautiful things that you can remember from your past. Concentrate for a second and remember one good experience from your past that you still talk about to this day. I'm already smiling about mine. It was a great day.

Everything about that day was on point. From the moment I woke up to the minute I fell asleep, that day was all about me. Can you remember an experience like that? Think about how you felt at that moment. Was your heart beating really fast or were you totally relaxed? Were you nervous and filled with anticipation? Did you have those ever so beautiful butterflies in your stomach? Were you indoors or outside somewhere? Can you remember the smells? What was around you? Were there other people there? I don't know about you, but I was only in the presence of one, and it was amazing. The emotions that had been building up inside of me exploded all at once, and that release was life-changing. It felt amazing! I had never experienced anything more incredible than that at that point in my life. Right in the middle of it, it seemed like the atmosphere was changing. I couldn't keep my eyes open, and the world just seemed different. I was turning into someone different. At that very moment, I was changed forever.

Reflecting on that perfect moment in my life has once again filled me with complete joy. I can't even wipe the smile off my face. I hold on tight to that memory because of how my whole day changes when I think about it. It gives me renewed energy. It gives me exactly what I need to change my current perspective on things where I can see situations more clearly and from a place of positivity. It's called reframing your thoughts and shaping your day.

Now that we have reframed our thoughts, let's go in the opposite direction and acknowledge that we have had some not so great days, weeks, months, and years. Some of us have literally had more bad days than good, and that is tragic. Who wants to continue living life like that? If you are done with the bad days, then you are in the right place.

The first step in doing away with bad days is saying "What's up" to them. Have a conversation with your bad days. Ask them how they are doing. Get really friendly and cozy with them and walk right up on them really close.

Now that you and your bad days are-face-to-face, looking each other straight in the eyes, take control and say "I'm done" to your bad days. Don't let your bad days get a word out, just keep telling them you're done, it's over, and you're ready for something new. Don't go back and forth debating with your bad days, let them know straight up that their time in your life has expired. Your bad days are going to try hard to grab hold of you and drag you back down that dark and lonely road, but don't let them touch you. This breakup is going to be very difficult for your bad days, and they desperately don't want to let you go, but its time. Allow your bad days to digest what's going on. You caught them off guard, so understand that the change is abrupt and uncomfortable, and your bad days really don't know how to function without you. It's kind of sad when you think about it. Empathize with your bad days and let them know that because of the time you spent with them, you know exactly how they are feeling right now. You and your bad days have been down for one another for a long time. Change is tough, but it's necessary for you to grow and move forward in life. Your bad days won't understand that but give them a second to realize you have had enough and you are serious this time. Everything that you and your bad days have gone through will forever be with you, but they will no longer define you. Today chains are being broken. Today you have decided to look straight ahead of you into the unlimited possibilities of your future. Today you are setting yourself free. Your relationship with your bad days is finally over.

Before you walk away from your bad days, let them know there are no hard feelings. As a matter of fact, thank them. Thank them because if it weren't for your bad days, you wouldn't be strong enough to accept the good days that are on the way. Thank them because they prepared you to know what to look out for when other bad days try to come your way and thank them for showing you that you deserve better. Take this time to say thank you! Tell them thank you for giving you the ultimate gift, which is the gift of testimony. Tell them thank you for showing you what it looks like when God keeps you through the worst of all situations. You may have felt like those bad days weren't fair, and you may have wanted to end it all, but you made it through because the plan for your life starts with the story your bad days gave you. Those bad days are not your enemy. They are your strength, your courage, and a testament to your faith. Remember everything from your bad days and find the lessons in them. You will need to use those lessons you have learned from your bad days to make your good days better than you could have ever imagined.

We have finally reached the end. Now, turn around and walk away from your bad days. No looking back over your shoulders, and definitely no turning around. You are safe now. No more harming yourself or letting those bad days harm you. Forgive yourself for allowing those bad days into your life. Forgive those bad days and those involved in those bad days for imposing on your life. You are finally free to release yourself from the feelings of guilt and anger. Release yourself from the pain of what was inflicted upon you. Release yourself from old things and old ways. Let's press the reset button and release ourselves from past hurt and heartache others have caused us and get excited about moving into a new day.

It is time to find out who you really are, where you are going, and how you are getting there. It is time to dig deep inside of your soul and pull out the new you. It is time to begin loving yourself and living your truth.

"People who are a big deal don't give themselves away cheaply." Sharon V. Dickey

Chapter 3

I'm a Big Deal

Sometimes people approach me, and clearly, by the games, they try to play, and the foolish words they utter from their mouths, they have no idea who I am. I try to give them the benefit of the doubt, so I just ask them straight out, "you don't know I'm a big deal, do you?" Like really? Who in their right mind, when they approach me have no idea that I am a big deal? I have been telling people I'm a big deal way before I got any of these letters and accomplishments behind my name and under my belt.

Those aren't even the things that make me a big deal. It's my Daddy's fault in case you have a problem with me believing I'm a big deal. He always told me, "you know you're smarter than C work," "you're so beautiful and chocolate," and my favorite, "no man is good enough for you." Then he would list all the reasons why whatever knucklehead I was interested in really was not good enough for me, which I could never argue with. Some people say I am a Daddy's girl and he got my head all swole up. I say yes! I am a Daddy's girl, and my father did an amazing job building up my self-esteem and self-confidence to prepare me for the obstacles I would face later in life that would try to beat me down, tear me apart, and completely break my spirit.

My mother took a different approach. She instilled independence in me. She would always say, "you don't need a man for nothing. You can be anything you want to be, and you can have anything you want to have, and you don't have to wait on a man to give it to you." In the sixth grade, when she started having these conversations about being independent with me, I had no idea why she thought it was important to tell me that. Once I stepped out into the world where I had to stand alone on my own, I remembered her words and saw how she was helping me stay on the right path to where when I was ready, I would be able to fly on my own and sore to heights she had never seen.

My parents' lessons were so intentional because they only wanted better than the best for me. My dad's arrogant approach and my mother's self-sufficient approach were the perfect combinations. Roll all of that together, add some sugar and spice, a pretty smile and an amazing personality and look out world! I am a big deal, and I have no intentions of letting you forget that! Love you, Mommy and Daddy!

What I want you to learn from this is that you are a big deal too. You must know it and believe it and feel comfortable walking in those shoes. You may not have had the family support like I had where I was able to learn this as a child. That is ok. As an adult, you have free will, and if you want some of this "I'm a big deal" belief that I have, then you can freely choose to borrow some of mine until you can build up your own. If someone has an attribute that you admire, and you would love to be that way, then borrow some of their energy and sunshine and make that attribute your own. For example, being optimistic isn't an attribute that everyone has. If you currently see the gloom and doom in everything, but you desire to know the joy and happiness in all things, then change the channel.

As an adult, you can shape your present and your future so that your past circumstances are no longer holding you back. I believe you can make a few adjustments here and tweak a couple of things over there and create a clear pathway to your future so that your past situations are no longer hindering you from obtaining the life full of abundance and Blessings that God has waiting for you! To do something new, you have to first learn something new. If your spirit has been broken and you have been beaten down by life and filled with negative images and ideas of yourself, then we need to spend some time rewiring your brain. Your automatic thoughts of yourself have to be "I am good enough!", not "am I good enough?" Here are a few lessons to help make you more aware of yourself on your journey to becoming a big deal.

Welcome to "I'm a Big Deal" 101 Training Class!

Lesson #1. Who are you? How would you even answer this question? Knowing who you are is vital if you want to be considered a big deal. Self-awareness and positive self-image are required. Having self-awareness means you know who you are. You know what you like and what you do not like. You know who you like, and who you do not like. Your values and principles are your own, meaning you make the rules for your life and you live life according to your own feelings, motives, and desires. There is no one else on this earth that is responsible for how you behave and interact with people. There is no "maybe," "I guess," or "I think so" in your vocabulary anymore. Your yes is your yes, and your no is your no. You are in complete control of you. Remember, the journey to discovering who you are can be challenging and it can take some time, but after you complete these lessons and finish reading this book, you will be well on your way.

   Having a positive self-image, feeling good about yourself and feeling confident in your own skin is another important step in becoming a big deal. What do you see when you look in the mirror? Do you even look in the mirror? I know what it is to purposely not have any mirrors in your bedroom. Stop hiding from the world. It's time to break free! Go find your nearest mirror. There's one in your bathroom, and there is one in your car. If there is no mirror where you are, then I want you to put a bookmark on this page and highlight this next sentence. Go to the dollar store and buy a mirror to keep on you at all times. Once you got your mirror in your hand, hold it up in front of your face and look at your face. What do you see? Do you see blemishes, scars, and skin discoloration, or do you see the beauty that God created? Seeing yourself as a beautiful human being perfect in every way is a belief that you have to have. It is called loving yourself. The same way you want others to love and adore you is the same way you have to love and adore yourself.

Lesson #2. Being a big deal involves having your life organized in a way that every decision you make moves you a step forward with everything properly aligned and in balance. Your personal life which includes your family and friends, your spirituality, career, finances, love life, health, and entertainment. Basically, you need to get your shit together. The road to "Getting your Shit Together-ville" is long and rough. It takes perseverance, hard work, dedication, and a lot of prayers to choose a path and stay on it. Lesson #2 is the most difficult, and it takes the most time because there are so many factors involved. This book will help you with Lesson #2. By the end of this book, you will have the tools you need to figure out who you are, where you are going, and what path to take to get there.

Lesson #3. To maintain your "big deal" status, you must keep upping your game. Five years ago, you were there, now you are here, and in five more years you will be up there. Set your sights on achieving new levels every year and never get comfortable where you are in life. Once you become comfortable, you no longer strive to be better. You become complacent and stagnated. There is no growth in complacency and stagnation. Maintaining the title of "big deal" means you must keep improving yourself and the people around you. Being a "big deal" is not a selfish thing. You have to learn how to help everyone around you become a "big deal" too.

One of my favorite quotes is "The best way to find yourself, is to lose yourself in the service of others", Mahatma Gandhi. Searching for your true self and being unafraid to live it is not an easy task. You have to have courage. You have to be bold. Those are the two main qualities for someone who is a "big deal." The easiest way to complete lesson #3 is to set annual goals and work hard to achieve those goals by the end of the year. Set your goals high and make sure they are things that you dream about. Your dreams are your true desires, and God will grant you your hearts desires if you ask him, believe He will do it, and have faith that He will. There is no quitting, getting discouraged, or giving up in "big deal" land. Striving to be your best you every day and looking toward improving your future is what solidifying your status as a "big deal" is all about.

"What have you done to be awarded or Blessed with a gift such as I?" Sharon V. Dickey

Chapter 4

What is Your Price of Admission?

We spent some time acknowledging our past and working on our self-awareness and self-esteem. The remaining chapters of this book will continue that work, but you should be feeling pretty good about yourself and the new direction you are taking in your life. So far, we have been focused solely on you, which is essential, but let's shift our focus a bit and take a look at our lives and how we allow other people to affect us on our journey to discovering who we are, where we are going and how we get there.

Take a moment, and ask yourself, who do you have in your life? A great way to find out if your friendships are real, tell your friends you are moving and ask them if they will help you pack and move. I am considering a move, and I was thinking, when I move, who do I have in my life that is going to help me box up all my items and load the U-Haul? I know my girls got my back, as they always do, but who else do I have that will not give me excuses for why they cannot help me? I challenge you to evaluate who you have in your life to support you and determine whether they are worth Your Price of Admission. What I mean by that is with all that you pay out to people, all that you give of yourself to comfort, protect and support them, what do you get in return? This is the Price of Admission into your life?

Sometimes it is much more comfortable, and basic human nature, to point out everybody and everything that is bothering you, everything and everyone that is keeping you from doing whatever you need to do, but the reality is that sometimes, we are the ones standing in our own way. We allow people to devalue us by not demanding those people to respect us, which leads to us having a lack of respect for ourselves.

In thinking about your life, discovering who you are, and working on building your personal relationship with God, who is that person, that you allow in your life, that is keeping you from honoring God? We all have something that we struggle with, something that we settle for that drops our Price of Admission. While you think about your Price of Admission deal breaker, I'll start by telling you about mine.

Married men for some reason love knocking at my door, and I fight hard not to be bothered with them. They try hard to gain your attention by rolling out the red carpet, five-star everything, which makes having them around seem beneficial and a welcome change to being alone. These men are 100% unavailable to you mentally, emotionally, and physically. They can never give you everything you need. They are never around to help pay any of your bills, oh wait, you do still have some that slide you a few extra dollars every now and then just enough to keep you thinking he is handling business or treating you special by going out his way to provide for you financially. Stop and think for a second what you had to put out and if you stop putting it out will the money flow as freely? Maybe, but probably not. So how much are you worth? What Is Your Price of Admission? Do you only cost your cell phone bill amount every month, so he can have control over being in communication with you? Maybe you are only worth the cost of your power bill? Even if he pays all the bills, including rent, he still ain't yours.

Oh wait, I forgot, he's separated, and he's going to get a divorce. We have friends, family members, even Hollywood stars who have shown us all in a very public manner that that old lie is just that no matter who you are. If you are worth having and providing for and supporting, then shouldn't this married/separated person be rushing to get the divorce finalized so they can be 100% yours? When I was ready to move on with my life, I filed for divorce in January, papers were served February 14th, and the divorced was finalized in April. When you are ready to put your past behind you, it doesn't take that long to get your business taken care of. Oh wait, they have assets, and let's not forget, it's cheaper to keep him or her. All of you are killing the game for everybody out here when you settle for less than what you are worth because people begin to believe if "I got away with it with this one, I can keep doing this to everyone I meet." I met that guy who jumped from woman to woman. He didn't trick me though. I knew from the jump that was his game. I just thought there was no way on God's earth, a person could swear the career they were pursuing was to enhance the kingdom of God and actually be a real live devil. I have seen the anti-christ yall. He's real. He'll look like he's being blessed, but when you ask questions and look closely, you will realize he is just juggling the funds of everyone he encounters. That's not called being Blessed, that's called being a hustler. We have to pay attention to the games we allow people to play with us. We have to begin nipping those behaviors in the bud and not let someone highjack months and years of our lives only to move on to their next sponsor. So how do you stop the madness? You begin by admitting to yourself that you have no idea how to determine your value making you ill-equipped to assess Your Price of Admission. Then, keep reading and move on to the next chapter.

Chapter 5

Un Poème…

"FINE As hell, but still Single as EVER!"

Why are you so pretty and single, you ask?

Hmmm, I thought.

Aha! Simple response, my brother

I'm pretty because…

My mocha skin is radiant, and I give it much care

My personality has a lot of flare

I walk upright and head high because I give reverence to God

I speak intelligently because my thoughts are of deeper substance and substantially involved

I intentionally build my character and mold myself to be someone I am proud of and an example to my loves

I stay focused and balanced, and that's all thanks to the good Lord above

I love a good joke, and my laugh is full of joy

Because I have given it to me and it's not yours to destroy

See all of these things make me pretty,

I agree with you, Shoot! I am!

But why am I single…

Hmmm, I thought

Aha! Simple response my brother

See, I've been broken

Yes, me with allll of my flyness

I

HAVE

BEEN

BROKEN

I've been broken and stripped of all that I THOUGHT I was in control of

I GAVE my joy away

I FORGOT how to laugh

MY FLARE was overshadowed by a dark cloud.

AND

I

JUST

DIDN'T

CARE!!

Then I looked at my LOVES!

MY LOVES!

Yes, I found purpose again

I found love again

I found peace again

And I found ME!

Now that I have me…

I REQUIRE an intelligent man with purpose and drive, my brother

I REQUIRE my car door to be opened, my brother

I REQUIRE romantic vacations and intimate staycations

I REQUIRE

I REQUIRE reverence for God and a brother that can throw down in the kitchen.

I REQUIRE handwritten letters that just say, "Hey Boo!"

Spontaneity, Creativity, Health Consciousness, oh these are just a few

I REQUIRE

Star quality father traits

A man that after 20 years of being with me, will still take me out on dates.

A provider, protector,

Oh, I could go on and on

But know, that I require for one main reason

I REQUIRE because I require all of these of myself.

And I REFUSE to accept anything less from someone else.

So, to answer your question simple and sweet,

Why someone as pretty as me is still single?

It's because I REQUIRE, my brother

I REQUIRE

Concept by: Sharon V. Dickey
Ghostwriter: ANC 4/14/2014

"You don't even qualify to try out for the team. Please take a seat in the bleachers." Sharon V. Dickey

Chapter 6

What is Your Worth?

We spent some time becoming aware of who we are and where our lives have brought us to this point. We understand how those experiences have affected us and shaped our character. We are more aware of our feelings, and we are focusing on what we desire in our lives. Now it is time to focus more on loving and respecting yourself and requiring others to do the same. Now you will begin to determine your worth.

Let's put a monetary value on your worth. How much

would you say you are worth per minute? How much is one minute of your time worth? Write that number down. Now multiply that number by 60. That's how much one hour of your time is worth. Now multiply that number by 24 and write that number down. That final total is how much you are worth per day. Label that number "My Daily Worth." Now let's take it a step further and multiply your daily worth by 90. Now, even if you made your per minute worth $1 per minute, 90 days of your time is still worth $129,600.

So in thinking about your daily worth, take a moment and reflect back on your past relationships. Have you ever dated anyone for 90 days whether it was 90 days straight or 90 days off and on? I can be honest and say I have dated several people for at least 90 days or more. As you continue to scroll through your past likes and loves, consider whether or not any of those people were literally "worth your time."

I have had one dating experience in my life, where to this day, I still believe that experience was priceless. The rest of them desperately needed a cap on my time. In my mind, I strongly believe I am worth $1000 per minute. That makes me worth $60,000 per hour, $1,440,000 per day and $129,600,000 for every 90 days I grace this earth with my existence and not one of those faces that flickered through my mind were even worth one minute of my time. As a matter of fact, I need to send out some bills requesting a repayment of my time, at the least for the first 5 minutes where they approached me. I'll eat the remaining minutes, days, months and even years because it was my lack of knowledge of my worth that created a situation where I allowed them to consume the rest of the time they lingered around in my life. I own my part in not understanding how valuable my time was back then. I own not attaching a price, a monetary value, to it and evaluating whether or not I was using my time wisely. Wasted time is equal to wasted money. We put a lot of value on money. Why not place that same value, if not more, on your time? You wouldn't waste money and frivolously throw it away, so why do we allow our time to be wasted and frivolously thrown away?

When you were with your past love, boo thang, fling, whatever, did every day you spent with them feel like you just treated yourself to your favorite five-star restaurant with the relaxing ambiance? Was it the most superb wine selection with someone waiting on you and catering to your every need with food perfectly prepared for you just the way you like it? Absolutely not because if you did, they wouldn't be an ex. One thing we don't do is throw away a perfectly good mate. I've heard so many times, and I've read so many places that old saying "one woman's trash is another woman's treasure." That's not true at all. No human is trash, and we shouldn't put so much value in man that we would classify them as a treasure. What we should do is recognize when a person is compatible or incompatible with us. Just because a man is incompatible with me doesn't mean that man is incompatible with the next woman. That is how we move in and out of relationships. Once your mate is no longer meeting your needs, you search for someone else to pick up where they fell off. The challenge is how much time we hold on to that person we are incompatible with. Stop and think about what made them incompatible in the first place. There were probably signs from the very beginning that either you did not pay attention to or you overlooked and brushed it off convincing yourself it wasn't really a big deal. We have been conditioned into thinking "nobody is perfect," and that "you'll have to put up with something no matter who you date or marry." That is true, but not completely. A person can be perfect. They can be perfect specifically for you. What I mean by "perfect specifically for you" is that what I find attractive you may find unattractive, or what doesn't bother me at all may bug the hell out of you. For example, for me, the things that I find as incompatible traits or things that bug the hell out of me, are things that I call deal breakers. My deal breakers outline traits I will not accept or entertain in my life. My deal breakers are like my shield of protection from foolery. They are a clear outline of my expectations and boundaries. No two people should expect their deal breakers to be the same. What I do not like, you may love, and that is ok. That is why we were created as unique individuals. My only advice would be to evaluate your deal breakers and make sure they are not superficial. Some things fall into a grey area. That area is called the "workable" zone. Please understand the workable zone is not the same as feeling like you'll have to put up with some mess just to keep a man. I'll give you an example of "workable" later. For now, let's work through this deal breaker thing by reviewing my list of deal breakers.

Deal breaker #1 – Hygiene

If your breath stank, you got about 30 seconds before I realize that offensive odor isn't something in the air, it is something in your mouth. I'll then be forced to cut you off mid-sentence and excuse myself from your presence. Don't nobody wanna smell all that! It simply is not cute. Hygiene, washing your hind parts daily, taking care of your body, seeing the dentist regularly and getting your dental work taken care of efficiently, is important to me. Using soap and water and following it up with some deodorant and some smell good is what I require. At 30 seconds you have now wasted $500 of my time. That is a new purse. That is a few new pairs of shoes. I can buy clothes for my babies, put food in the frig and pay a bill too if I budget right. I cannot allow someone who is off gate clearly showing signs of incompatibility to stand in front of me and as the clock keeps ticking the toilet keeps flushing down hundreds and thousands of dollars which is the value I place on my time. No, stank you!

Sometimes proper hygiene can be hidden, especially if you are in the world of online dating. That's a whole other chapter I might get to later. For now, I am speaking about the guy that walks up to you in the bar when you are there at happy hour with your co-workers or your girls. That dude that sees you in the mall and gets up the courage to come over to you and tell you, you have a beautiful smile. That dude. For me, that dude usually is handicapped or special needs. Ask my sister. I am not lying to you. I get the dudes who have an arm deformity, drooling, and walking with a limp that approach me all too often. All jokes aside, I know I have a compassionate spirit, and I knew way back in high school that I had a soft place in my heart for the special needs population, but I do not want to date or marry into it. I am not knocking it. Love who you want. It's just a personal deal breaker for me.

Deal breaker #2

Well, maybe that was two, lol! We'll skip along to number three.

Deal breaker #3 – Physical Appearance

This deal breaker is physical appearance. Here we go. Don't start on me, please. I am not superficial so hear me out before you cast judgment on me. Ridicule me after I explain my position on physical appearance. I am speaking of what I see on your physical body when I stand in front of you and look at you. We do not take the time to survey people when they present themselves to us. So, do this, imagine a guy walks up to you and says hello. Stop right there! Press pause and stop the world. Envision that person and everything surrounding them frozen in time except for you. Take a moment and survey that person bottom to top. Their feet would be up first. Are they wearing sneakers, flip flops, boots? Are they dirty, raggedy, or crisp looking and brand new? This may sound shallow but surveying a person from foot to head can give you indicators on how much time you should allow that will either count as an investment or just those toilet flushing sounds. Their feet and how they are dressed is important. Please understand, it is not about brand names and things like that. It is more of a mental process I am considering in this area and also looking for clues that lead to bigger issues. For example, in my situation, had I paid more attention to the foot region, I would have noticed the left shoe sole was about 2-3 inches higher than the right shoe sole. With my track record, that is a clear indication that I need to proceed with caution. This person may be picking up on my compassionate energy, and I may need to see where I can offer some resources and redirect them. My personal preference for the foot area can be many things. I love men who can wear those cloth flip flops as the surfers do. Now what I have settled for in the past, because I lacked clarity on this foot-to-head surveying process is two feet in Jesus sandals—so to speak—looking like he been playing soccer with some rusty old sweet potatoes in a clay dirt field. This is why it is so important to start from the bottom to the top because the top might be on point and we get distracted and miss out on the clear signs of incompatibility also known as deal breakers. Let's just say you don't mind two rotten potatoes for feet and move on up scanning from the ankle to the neck. That is a large area to cover, but it can be scanned quickly. There's nothing really specific you are looking for, but make sure you pay attention to what is important to you.

You may be at the gym, the beach, the grocery store, or volunteering somewhere so that person can be dressed in many different ways. My personal preference is neat and clean. If your pants are sagging below your butt and I can see stains on your boxers, then that quick scan just saved me a lot of time and money. But let's just say booboo stained jockeys are sexy to you. To each his own, do you and keep scanning upwards. Focus your attention on the shirt area. Are they wrinkled when your outfit and where you are located constitutes a need to have used an iron this morning? Maybe they are wearing gym clothes. Are you at the gym, just left the gym, going to the gym, or are you at a night club and you are wearing a little black dress and some cute heels? The point is, that person doesn't match their environment which makes me wonder what is going on in their head. It's not like you stopped by the grocery store or somewhere to run a few errands before you went home. They are literally dressed and out for a nice evening looking like Fat Albert in a tight red sweat suit thinking that is okay. Not sexy and a clear indicator of incompatibility for me. Let's keep moving upwards. The only area left on the body is the head, the arms and the hands which we skipped. Some people have a thing about hands. Dirty nails mean you are an unclean person is what I have heard most. Here is that "workable" zone I was talking about. Maybe dude works in construction, or maybe he's a mechanic or has some other job where he works with his hands. Some things can be resolved with a one on one conversation and a serious look on your face to let them know you are serious and you expect an immediate change. This really shouldn't be a deal breaker because it can be easily worked out. However, if you deem something as "workable," set a time limit as far as how long after the conversation you expect the issue to be rectified. For dirty nail guy, give him some nail clippers and a side eye and continue on about your lives. If you absolutely cannot tolerate something that others may see as "workable" then don't stress yourself and put it in the deal breaker basket. I completely understand if the "workable" zone can be tolerated easier if dirty nails were on Mr. tall, dark, with a six-pack, versus them being on Mr. short, stubby, and cockeyed. I get it, and I won't judge your deal breakers if you don't judge mine. Another example of "workable" would be hairstyles. If you like bald men, it's ok to date a guy with locs. Check his hairline. He might be bald sooner than you think. The main point for the "workable" zone is understanding all of those things are transformable. Just remember always to be careful and understand that nitpicking is not equal to deal breakers. Now I know you are waiting for me to go over the deal breaker for the head region, but honestly, I don't have a deal breaker for that area. Beauty is in the eye of the beholder.

Now that we have taken the time to survey the potential suitor, now it is time to listen to what they have to say. Sometimes, we don't take the time to scan the physical appearance properly, that smile made you melt, they started talking, and you still stuck on the smile and haven't heard a word they said. Next thing you know, you exchange numbers, and there you go off to wasted time land. Let's back it up to my final deal breaker.

Deal breaker # 4 - Conversation

My dream is to grow old with someone and be able to sit on the porch and just enjoy conversing with that person. Is your conversation compatible with mine? Can we talk about nothing and everything until 3am like we are back in high school? Do we talk about the things that we love and agree to disagree peacefully on everything else? Do you make me laugh so hard that my face hurt? If we cannot be content with enjoying one another's company, then that would be a deal breaker for me.

Knowing your worth and making a guideline to keep you on track for what you do and do not like can help keep you from wasting so much of your valuable time. Being able to list your deal breakers should empower you to be comfortable with what is pleasing to you. Be empowered to love who you want to love and not worry about what anybody else thinks. Be honest with yourself when making your list. If you like the boogeyman, then fine, the boogeyman is yours. You love and adore his raggedy ass, and you bet not complain not one time about how he's not good enough. But if you are 1000% sure that you prefer a more refined man, then that preference is yours to have. Just remember, if your list of deal breakers ends up having the same number of items as your monthly grocery list, then you may need to do a little bit of self-evaluation and ask yourself, are these things on my list really that serious, or could I be unconsciously sabotaging myself out of fear? Fear of happiness is a real thing, and fear will keep you in a box. It is time to break free and finally love and accept who you are and be confident in your likes and dislikes and steadfast in what you will and will not accept in your life. God will send you the desires of your heart. Begin to love yourself as you desire to be loved. Then take a step back and get out of your own way.

> "I'm not adding any un-accomplishments to my list of goals. If you don't belong in my life for specific reasons, then you won't be allowed to hang on my coattail."
>
> Sharon V. Dickey

Chapter 7

Pinky Toe

When my daughter was still a baby only a few months old sleeping in my very comfy king size bed, although it was just her and me in that big ole bed, she always had to be touching me in some way. I was a new mommy and scared I would roll over and crush her so once she fell peacefully asleep, I would slide her away from me, so I could finally get some peaceful sleep, but she would always find her way right back under me. So, I would slide her over again, and she'd scoot right back under me, and I would slide her away further, and one day instead of her finding her way back under me, she put just her leg on me. That was better than her whole body, but at this point, I was beginning to understand that my baby was just wanting to be close to me. For her safety and my peace of mind, I moved her leg off me. This time she waited until I dozed off, and of course, I was awakened when she put her leg back on me. Fearing I had rolled over onto my baby, I woke up panicked, then I immediately noticed I was still in the exact same spot, and she had just thrown her leg back on me. In my new mommy mind, at this point, I was battling for personal space, so I could get some sleep and not be worried that I broke my child's leg in the middle of the night, so I moved her leg off of me again. She put it right back on me. This time I slid her leg off me where she wasn't touching me anymore, but I could still feel the warmth of her body heat and even that wasn't good enough. She slid her foot back enough to where the whole bottom of her foot was touching me. I pushed her foot off me. She put it back on me. I pushed her foot off me again, then she waited a bit and stuck just her toes on me. I couldn't help but laugh, and since I was wide awake at 3am why not keep playing the push-Amiya-foot-away game, so I pushed her toes off me, and she put them right back on. Now, I'm committed to winning this battle, and I push her toes off me again. Then, slowly I feel her foot moving back towards me, and she gently places one toe on me. I said, "Really Amiya!" LOL! One toe and it was her pinky toe at that. I pushed that sharp pinky toe off me, and again, slowly she put that one toe back on me. Not ready to give up, I pushed her pinky toe off me again and vowed to do something about that toenail that was about to cut me like a knife in the morning, and immediately she put it right back on me. It started out with her whole body, then her leg, and now the smallest part of her body and it was torturing me. So, I cut my lamp on, and I looked down and saw the cutest little tiny toe resting on my forearm. Only a new mommy can fall in love with a pinky toe cutting through your skin at 3:30am. I opened the drawer on my nightstand and pulled out my fingernail clippers. This was an adult toenail on this baby foot cutting me, and I needed adult nail clippers to handle this job. I clipped the tip of her toenail off and rubbed my finger across it to make sure it was smooth. What was concerning about the entire time I was going through this battle, was that she never woke up. Even when I cut the light on and cut her nail, she never opened her eyes. I believe she was playing possum, as my mother would say, but either way, I soaked in my new mommy moment with my baby, and I cut my lamp off and slid her whole body to the middle of my bed because my competitive spirit just couldn't let it go. I waited for the game to resume, but she didn't make her way back towards me. Finally, I could relax and get some sleep. A few hours later, the sun was rising and shining through my bedroom curtains. The sun painfully awakened me like sharp knives stabbing me in my eyes. I was so exhausted, but I quickly looked over to make sure Amiya was still breathing and fast asleep--she was. She had scooted closer to me, but her whole body wasn't under me. Feeling like I had won the battle and had established clear sleeping boundaries, I went to move my arm, and there it was. The softest little pinky toe was gently touching my arm. The unconditional love you receive from your baby is amazing and them wanting to be close to you even if it's just the tiniest softest touch of a pinky toe can only be adored by a new mommy. As my heart melted, it dawned on me that I had secretly lost the battle at some point within the last few hours while I slept peacefully. And there you have the concept of the pinky toe.

Now, when that pinky toe is attached to a big rusty

crusty foot of a grown adult, it's not so cute anymore but keep that visual in your head for a moment. Who have you been in bed with then soon you find you are unable to get from underneath their pinky toe? Who was it that with all of their great and wonderful attributes, they were so bad for you, and instead of shutting them out of your life completely, they always found a way back to you? That's pinky toe. People will treat you the way that you allow them to treat you. Before understanding that my worth is technically priceless, I remember, this guy I dated after I graduated college. To this day, he is the only guy I dated that I knew I would have married if he just would have gotten his shit together. He's the first and last man I'll ever live with without being married to. We were great together and so flawed together all at the same time. We were functionally dysfunctional. I remember he got off work an hour before me. I would come home after a long day of being a customer service representative apologizing to people who were complaining about nothing for eight hours, and he would be standing in the kitchen with some shorts and a tank top on cooking dinner. He had the most beautiful salt and pepper silky, wavy hair that would still be a little damp and glistening from his after-work shower. His cologne smelled so good. I couldn't get enough of his bowed legs. Plus, his feet were so cute! They were smooth, and his toes were perfect, and he kept his toenails cut and clean. I can't skip over his smile. That's how he got me. His teeth were white and perfectly aligned although he never wore braces. Aesthetically, he was beautiful to me. He worked with his brother who owned his own landscaping business, and he had his own car and apartment when we met. Not only was he very attractive to me, employed and mobile, but that boy could cook his behind off! A man that can cook is number one on my list. He could fry some chicken so perfectly it was like I was dreaming while I was eating, and his rice was perfectly cooked with no grains sticking together. I will never forget the first time he cooked for me. It was fried chicken, green beans and plain white rice. I was looking at the rice wondering where the gravy was, and then he brought the butter over and put a slither of it over my hot smoking rice. That cold butter instantly melted all over that perfect rice. It tasted just like my Grandma Maggie butter rice. I was in love! The package that was presented to me was all it took. I was so happy! Then the honeymoon ended, and shit got real. My perfect package and I used to barhop with my bestie and his brother. After a few outings, I noticed that after about three beers his eyes would start crossing up and he would begin to slur and stagger, but those times he went home with his brother. This particular night we were out barhopping playing pool and having a great time. After two beers, I suggested he stop there and babysit that second beer because he was still real chill with that level of consumption. Apparently, me offering that bit of responsible advice offended him, and he far exceeded the three beers I'm normally around him long enough to see. Here we go with the eyes crossing up, slurring, and staggering all over the place. Quickly, accusations of me liking and wanting to be with other men in the bar started flying out his mouth. I hadn't even noticed the other men in the bar. I was not paying attention to them, and they were not paying attention to me. If anything, all eyes were on him looking like a drunken fool cuttin' up in the bar. He wouldn't let the accusations go. His brother tried to stop him from talking stupid. My bestie tried to stop him. At this point he was ruining everybody's good time, so we left. I had parked at his house which was in the same neighborhood my bestie lived in. His brother drove all of us from the bar to his house so I could get my car and I would drop my bestie off at her house around the corner. The whole time in the car he was in and out of being really sweet and sappy with me apologizing for his behavior, wanting to hug and kiss on me, but when I refused his affection, he would go right back to the unwarranted claims of infidelity. By the time we got home, I had had enough, and I was done being in a relationship with this insecure dude that can't hold his alcohol. I got out of the car and slammed the door and headed straight for my car. He started with the apologies again. I had no more patience to listen to him, so I ignored him, unlocked my car and got inside. My bestie and his brother were standing on the sidewalk talking. He had followed me to my car. When I got inside, I closed and locked my door and cranked up the car. He was beating on my window talking about how sorry he was. He walked around to the passenger side of my car and tried to open the door, but of course, it was locked too. He was yelling for me to open the door, but I refused. I cracked my window and asked his brother to drop off my bestie, and he said he would. I put my car in reverse and began slowly backing up as I yelled at the drunk still knocking on my passenger window to move out the way because I was leaving. He was still begging me not to leave, but I was shaking my head no, refusing to stay so he said, "alright then, "F" you, I don't care no way!" as he staggered clumsily around the parking lot toward the sidewalk. It was like the world stopped and everything was silent and frozen in time. That was the first time he had ever cursed at me. Although he technically did not call me a vulgar, nasty name, in my mind the "F" word turned into the "B" word, and at that moment, the aggressiveness of the use of that "F" word made it feel like he was calling me out of my name, and the shock of it took me somewhere I could not easily return from. I remember it still, 20 years later, as if it happened yesterday. I went from disappointment and upset with myself for my poor choice in a mate, to hearing whispers of "murder murder, kill kill" in my ear, also known as going from "0 to 100". I immediately felt numb, and all I saw was red. I rolled my passenger window down and asked him "what did you say to me?" because clearly, I had to have heard him wrong. This drunken fool repeated it and added "leave! Get on out of here!" to it. Now I'm seeing redder. So, I said, "I bet you won't say it again!" He came closer to my car and said, "I said get the "F" on outta here!" Without thinking, I put my car in drive, and I tried to hit him, but he jumped back a little when he saw my headlights beaming in his direction, and I missed the intended direct hit. My right front tire caught a piece of him though. That tire was resting gently on top of his foot, and when I felt the bump, I knew I had rolled onto some portion of his body, so I stopped right there. I said, "Say it again!" He started yelling "you on my foot!". My bestie started yelling "Sharon! You're on his foot, backup!" I said, "Hell No! He out there talking all that shit! Imma run over his ass again!" Then I drove forward a little bit, put the car in reverse and backed up over his foot again. I stopped long enough to put my window all the way down to tell him what he could kiss then I sped off and went home.

I thank God for moving him out of the way because had I hit him with my car, I could have killed him, and my life would be very different right now. Looking back, I was way too young for the life I was living. I had just graduated college, I was a very confused 22-year-old who even with a bachelor's degree and graduating with honors, I still had no idea of my own worth or what I was going to do with my brand-new life. I should have been focused on continuing my education and going to Norfolk State to get my master's degree which was my initial plan before I met that knucklehead. Instead, after this clear moment of insanity, I decided it would be a great idea to continue dating, and later shacking-up with this man who was 9 years my senior. I own that, though. That was the choice that I freely made against my parents' will, and I learned a very valuable lesson from the consequences that followed for the next two years that I continued to stay and play a part in his drama.

I shared this personal out-of-control moment of my life with you to try and explain the importance of knowing your worth, having confidence in your own abilities, and respecting yourself. When you don't have those things, then you leave yourself open and vulnerable to where people can take advantage of you, abuse you, and break you. I've gone through the break up then get back together again only to break up again and get back together again madness. Every time you break up, it's a traumatic moment in your life where you remember it just like it was yesterday, too. Unfortunately, I am not the only one who went blank and tried to hit someone with a car. Unfortunately, I am not the only one who had to pack up, sneak and leave in the middle of the night so that my leaving or abandoning them didn't trigger their anger, which would lead to a fight I knew I would lose, or I knew this last time if I didn't leave right then, I would win.

Don't be fooled by the pinky toe thinking it is cute because this person or people like him, keep giving you attention and coming back around to string you along and waste more of your valuable time. They have a hold on you in some way that you are allowing. They know you are a big deal. They are aware of your worth. Either they are hanging around you to use you for all that you can give them until you have nothing left to give to them or to yourself, or they are trying to stay close enough to you until they can get themselves together. What will happen then? You have no way of knowing. We would hope they would be everything you have ever dreamed of and the two of you go off and live happily ever after. That is a possibility. It is also a possibility that they leave and take their new, well put-together self on to the next person. Either situation is not beneficial to you. It messes with your emotions and throws off your mind, body, and spirit balance. As a result of their foolishness time and time again, repeating the same ole mess over and over, you may be praying harder and increasing your spirituality, which was my case. Prayer got me out of that situation and finally being tired and fed up helped as well. What suffered was my body and my mind. I gained the most weight I have ever weighed during that relationship because I was so miserably unhappy and didn't know how to leave or maybe I just couldn't muster up the strength to leave this man who I thought was the one. This was the only relationship I have ever been in where I felt the symptoms of depression. My mental health was severely affected. I felt like I was in a state of confusion all the time, and I was having issues with anxiety because sometimes he would stop and drink on the way home from work, so I never knew what was coming through that door. The only thing constant was him telling me he loved me every day, drunk or sober, so much so that I did really believe him. I remember saying to myself constantly, "I know he loves me so why won't he just stop drinking?" All he had to do was one simple thing, right? Stop drinking. That's it. I wasn't asking for anything complicated. Or at least at that time, I didn't think I was asking for too much. Love should trump everything, right? I love you, then just stop smoking. I love you, then just stop eating yourself to death. I love you, then just stop cheating on me. I love you, then just stop gambling away all of our money. I love you, then just get a divorce. "Then just" is easy to say for the person who's requiring more from their mate. The other side to that is when you don't get compliance from your "then just", you must recognize that you do know you are worth more than what you are getting; however, you may not feel ready to own up to the choice you made early on after you ran over his foot to stay with him. That choice got you where you are today. How much more can you take? How much longer will you stay on this merry-go-round?

When it comes to relationships, there is one thing to keep in mind. A pinky toe situation doesn't help you in any way become greater. You can't build anything with it, and you can't grow with it. Anybody that you allow to be in your space should be required in some way to help make you great. That is the type of people you want around you. People who are pushing you forward, not holding you suspended in space. The people you hang around shape your character and influence your behavior. Make sure you only allow people in your life who continuously encourage and inspire you to be better today than you were yesterday. Vet your friend's list and only keep the people who are going to push you forward. For that mate that has you wrapped around their pinky toe or the one that every time you try and leave them and put them in your past, they always find a way to get right back up in your face, it is time to release yourself from the grip of the pinky toe.

Remember your worth. You have to pick yourself up and get to work on building up your confidence and your self-esteem. God will give you everything that you need to help you move forward. Being honest with yourself enables you to discover yourself, and it sets you on a journey to knowing yourself. When you say, "I know who I am," that means you are confident in who God has created you to be. You accept all of your faults and flaws, and you stop repeating old habits because you no longer have to depend on other people to tell you your worth. There is no way to move forward if you keep walking towards your past. Set your boundaries, stick to your guns, and start thinking about your purpose. It is time to start breaking free.

"I'm not up for any trickery or foolery. I only date with intention. If you don't have any honorable intentions, then intend on leaving me be." Sharon V. Dickey

Chapter 8

How to Get Rid of a Man with No Intentions

Invite him to Church. Most men will ignore the invitation and scurry on to the next woman who doesn't require a Godly man in her life. If he's a real devil like the one I allowed in my life, he will accept your invitation, show up bright and early and roll right up in Church with you. For this reason, I cannot end this chapter right here as I had planned.

If you got a cunning devil, here is what you need to look out for. Once you get inside the church, go sit as close to the front row as possible. After he sits down, wait about 10 minutes and check to see if he is fidgeting. Then lean back and check his collar for smoke, cause he's about to burst into flames any minute now. Pay attention to his body language to see how uncomfortable he is with being in the house of the Lord. He may talk to you and try to crack a joke when clearly it's time to be quiet because the Pastor is praying. He may start fanning with the program, or you may notice he's reading it for the fifth time. The words have not changed. It still says Sunday school is at 9:30am immediately following the first service. 9:30, not 10:30. You read it right the first four times. Is he crossing and uncrossing his legs repeatedly? Is he constantly rubbing his pants like he's trying to get the wrinkles out of them, or brushing that invisible lent off? Did he pull out a piece of gum yet? I sure hope you are old school AME Zion and it's the adult missionary Sunday to usher. Just let Sis. Green get him. His day is about to change for the worse!

This type of dude is despicable coming up in the house of the Lord knowing good and well he doesn't want anything serious nor long term, and surely not permanent with you. Don't feel obligated to force a man to have a personal relationship with God. Focus on your own personal relationship with God. Taking the time to work on your personal relationship with God will make you stronger, and it will give you the confidence you need to face any situation. You will be able to see how worthy you are of something greater, and the self-respect that you gain by developing this relationship with God will improve your self-esteem all the way around. My advice would be to stay clear of the "take him to Church" test run. Instead, fast and pray and wait for God to give you the answer about this guy and save yourself the embarrassment of all the Church folk talking about you. Confidence, self-respect, and knowing your worth are required for you to continue developing and moving forward towards your goal. Sometimes being in a relationship and having a mate is a wonderful thing, and sometimes it can be the daily distraction that is hindering you from achieving your goals. You may have to decide if you are strong enough to be in this dating game while you are working on building your confidence and self-esteem. Being in the dating game opens you up to meeting many no-intention men who can affect any progress you have made towards self-improvement. At this time, the focus should be on you and doing things that make you happy and are pleasing to God. I'm not insinuating that dating is not in God's plan for you, but I think it is essential to understand how to protect your heart and all the progress you have made in discovering who you are so you can keep pushing forward. At this stage, if you choose to date, at least put your boxing gloves on.

"If you find yourself saying he sounds so perfect and I can't believe he's real, proceed with caution."

Sharon V. Dickey

Chapter 9

Stranger Danger!

Dating sites and dating apps are still popular and the most convenient way to meet many different people from all over the country by just swiping left or right. I won't spend much time on this topic, but I know many of you are still checking the app to see how many messages you got from God knows who behind that handsome profile picture, so here we go.

One thing to keep in mind about this dating game is that it can knock you off your own game. After you have been broken and now going through the process of building yourself back up, you have to be very careful of who you give your energy to. If you give it to the wrong person, it could completely knock the wind from under your sail and send you crashing back down to the bottom all over again. As humans, we desire to love and be loved. Dating is just a natural part of the process, and if you desire to find your true mate, then there is no other way but to start dating. Just don't jump into dating too soon. Take some time for yourself to become confident in who you are and what you like and don't like. Wait until you have developed very clear boundaries and have learned how to set expectations for what you will and will not accept. Dating is very complex with all the emotions and feelings of vulnerability floating around getting in the way. You have to have a game plan. If you must start dating again, remember to take your time with it. Dating websites are convenient and just the way of the world right now. I have tried internet dating many times on many different sites, and I have failed miserably. The internet is full of people who have real intent on finding love, no intention on finding love but saying in their profile that's what they want, and people looking to take advantage of you in any way they possibly can. I have encountered them all, mainly people trying to take advantage of me. My favorite loser was the one that called himself a Christian who at 40 was still trying to be a gospel rapper. Unfortunately, I no longer put forth my energy to develop other people's dreams. While you are utilizing all of your resources, exerting all of your energy going hard for them, being everything and doing everything to help them be successful, your own dreams are sitting on the sideline collecting dust. Dream for yourself, set your personal goals, and focus on you and as you achieve your dreams and reach your goals, people who are doing the same will gravitate towards you, and you will notice how you will be able to identify all the liars and people with evil intent who cross your path more easily and clearly.

My advice for internet dating would be to approach it with a nothing to lose attitude. If you meet someone nice who entertained you with conversation and made you smile and feel special, then just simply enjoy that moment with no expectations for it to ever happen again. Treat each encounter as an opportunity to meet new people, possibly network, but be very cautious about building a future with them. Make sure you are not being catfished, and facetime or live video chat no later than the third conversation to avoid wasting valuable time. Never forget your worth. Look out for red flags, like if they can't talk to you on the phone outside of their working hours. If they text only and never call you at all, those are definitely the dudes that are strictly for entertainment purposes at your leisure only. If they only talk about themselves, remember you are not billing them for therapy hours. Don't allow this person to steal your mental energy. Go sit on your own couch and have a conversation with God and deal with your own problems. Be suspicious of the guy who is 40 and over and has never been married. There is a reason why nobody has snatched him up. The biggest one I would say to look out for is the separated guy whose wife is the blame for their marriage not working. He will keep trying to assure you he is going to leave his wife to keep you hanging on. Consider all that you give to this person concerning what you receive. If you desire to be a side chick, then enjoy your unavailable mate. If you desire to be a wife, make your expectations clear, guard your heart, and keep it friendly.

Take what you can use from my experiences and create a force field around you. I'm pretty sure your experiences will not be much different than mine, but you have the advantage in the situation because now you have the probability of what is going to happen before you enter into the situation. Keep an eye out for the cues and clues in the behaviors of the people you meet online. If you cut things off before you get in too deep, these new experiences will strengthen your character and build up your confidence to where you can trust yourself to make the best choices for your life. Working on building a personal relationship with God will help tremendously in this area too. Start by simply talking to God. Have a conversation with Him just like you would with anyone else. Spending alone time with Him having conversations about who He wants you to be, and the direction He wants you to go in life will open the door to start building that relationship. Since you are already on the internet swiping left and right, open up a new page, do some research and find out what God's promises for your life are. You can always hold God to His Word. That dude you met on the internet which in his profile said, "my word is my bond," might be your 40-year-old gospel rapper, and soon enough he'll show you how good his word is.

"If God has snatched someone out of your life, trust the process and let them stay gone. Find comfort in knowing it is for your good." Sharon V. Dickey

Chapter 10

Ghosted Again?

So, you've been working on yourself, and you're trying to do this "building a personal relationship with God" thing I keep talking about, but you're not sure if it is working. Maybe you're thinking God ain't feeling you like that because things are not changing in your life. For a moment you figured you'd give it a try and you felt like God was listening to you and you thought y'all were good, but some time has passed and it seems like God has "ghosted" you just like some of the people in your life have done before. I had a situation where I met this guy who at first seemed to be perfect. He was brilliant. The type of guy that could speak intelligently about any topic especially world events and cultural awareness. He was health conscious and mixed his herbs and made his healthy recipes just like I did. He was very confident and sure of himself, and his spirituality was on point. We talked on the phone a lot. We could talk for hours about anything and everything and often made four hours talking until two or three in the morning seem like 15 minutes. We had so many things in common and sharing my hopes and dreams and struggles with him was easy and comforting. We both have a strong personal relationship with God, so whenever one was going through something, we took the time to go to war praying for the other openly in each other's presence together. Sometimes I would start, and he would finish, or he would start, and I would finish, and we both would be ready to shout by the time the praying was over. To listen to me tell our story, you would think we dated for years, when in fact, it only lasted about 45 days. I started noticing he was distancing himself. For some reason, something had changed. I didn't know why or what was going on, but I felt in my spirit he was struggling with something. He began ignoring my texts or responding hours later. I would call at any time of the day, and where he used to answer, now he won't even return my calls. We had shared everything and promised we would maintain an open and honest relationship. And then the day came where there was no phone call initiated by either of us. I waited. Then the next day, the same thing. I waited. The days began to add up, and the silence began to hum loudly. So, I text one last prayer that God would protect him and guide him through whatever he was going through, and still no response. Just like that, days of silence turned into weeks and months of pain and despair. He literally disappeared out of my life. I never heard from him again.

Unfortunately, this guy I am describing isn't just one guy. He's multiple guys. The thing that got me though was realizing I was the only constant thing in all of those stories. When you have been ghosted, you begin to think about that relationship or that encounter and evaluate everything you did and everything you said and what he said back trying to find either a miscommunication, a misunderstanding, or some other piece of evidence that proves whatever went wrong, that you must have missed entirely, warranted this disappearing act. You've checked all of the text messages, and you've listened to all the voicemails, and you cannot find one thing that sounds like it could have been taken the wrong way, so you have nothing concrete to stand on as the reason why you just got ghosted. As your soul stirs and you're up all night tossing and turning, and your mind begins to get a little cloudy and confused, you still have to find somebody to blame for the abrupt ending to this perfect fairytale. It's unfathomable as to how someone who you seemed to get along with so well has just up and left without a trace. You are sitting in the room all by yourself, and you hear that voice say, "is it me?" "did I do something wrong?" How do I keep getting ghosted? I was utterly fed up and sick and tired of being given a glimpse of a dream-come-true fairy tale like relationship only to hear crickets chirping in the background a month or two later. I know my personal relationship with God is on point, and I am doing everything I am supposed to do so why does this ghosting thing still keeps happening to me?

On this last ghosting experience, I decided to take all of the emotion that was distracting me out of it and place it on a wall like a map so I could take a step back and look at the whole picture and not just snapshots of the happy moments. As I stood staring at this bigger picture, I was reminded that because I am good with God and I actively work on building our relationship and not being a Martha, I know that everything He does in my life is only for my good. Even when the thing I am going through does not feel good at all and is very uncomfortable and not something I want to deal with again, that uncomfortable thing is only for my good.

I began to think back to all the prior ghostings, and I realized I was blaming God for placing someone in my life that looked like a great candidate for my future just to have it turn out that they were just like all the rest of these no-intention men that always seem to keep coming my way. Now, I had a very long conversation with God, and I asked, no, I desperately begged for him to please, do not send another one of His children my way unless they are who I am supposed to be with for the rest of my life. I had the nerve to tell God I was done with all the lessons and that I did not need to learn anything else about heartache and broken promises and that I was good on that topic. So, I told Him I would depend solely on Him and for him to make it clear when somebody was just passing through so I would know not to get attached. After this deep plea with God, still, these no-intention men keep coming my way. The ghostings continued to occur, but not as often as they used to because I learned how to make better choices by using the principles in this book I am now sharing with you. Nevertheless, they still came.

Still standing in front of this wall reflecting back on the bigger picture of these disappearing acts and completely baffled by their purpose, I decided it was time for another heart to heart with my Heavenly Father about these occurrences. I asked God "WHY do you keep letting this happen to me?" I know some of you just threw this book across the room, but prayerfully the Holy Spirit told you to go pick it back up and let me explain. Most of us have been condition and "Bible bullied" into thinking we are never to question God which I believe is ridiculous. How can you have a conversation with someone and gain an understanding if you don't ask questions? How can I work on our relationship if I am scared to have an honest conversation with Him? I believe God wants me to ask Him why. I believe that because when I do ask Him Why our conversations get really deep and it takes our relationship to another level. My curiosity brings us closer. We spend more time together where I am in His presence, and we are actively engaging one another. I spoke of being a Martha earlier. I was listening to my siSTAR Elder Precious Bernard speak at an event, and she said "Martha invited Jesus into her home; however, she did not entertain Him because she chose her responsibilities over His presence. She was present but not in His presence."

Every day I make sure I am spending time in God's presence making time for just the two of us to grow closer together. That helps to build my personal relationship with

Him. For this ghosting situation, I needed an answer. I'm a tough cookie, but these ghostings were beginning to wear on me, and they were starting to compromise my Faith. In those moments, I ask why because my Faith is all I have, and I don't allow anything to mess with it, so there are times when God and I have to have a Q&A and address issues like this ghosting thing. I needed to know how God gives me everything I want and answers all of my prayers but seemingly ignores this one thing. I had asked why several times before, but at this moment as I stood staring at the bigger picture on the wall, He finally answered me. He revealed to me that the person He sent my way needed something that only I could give them to enhance their walk with Christ and increase their faith to become a true believer. He said "They did not ghost you. I placed them in your life, and I allowed them to stay until they got what I needed them to get. Once that need was met, they did not need any more of your precious time, so I snatched them out your life so they would not take their mess, that I did not show you, and disrupt the calling I have for you to fulfill". I am about to shout typing this right now! Be careful when you say, God, I surrender all and use me for your will because sometimes His work may feel uncomfortable. His work is not in the safe zone. His work doesn't always feel good, but His work is always intentional and purposeful. God has a calling on your life and sometimes that calling requires selflessness and sacrifice.

Sometimes, when God snatch someone out of our lives, we go running behind them chasing them down and doing everything we can to get them to come back to us. When you chase them down and pull them back into your life, you are extending that expiration date God set for them to have. Like old milk, when you keep somebody in your life beyond their expiration date, you might find yourself wishing you hadn't because now everything in your house and your life is all funked up. Remember, what God has for you is yours, and it won't just up and disappear on you out of nowhere one day. Ghosting, or someone's abrupt exit from your life, is intentional and part of God's purpose. Allow it to happen, and don't look at it as a bad thing anymore. It is not meant to break your spirit; it is meant to build the Kingdom.

Chapter 11

Un Autre Poème...

"I'll Do Fine If I Just Be Me"

I was trying to decide what type of poet should I be.

Should I be sister girl power to the people

Should I be lady superhero and save all my lost sisters

Should I be madam intellect and mesmerize you with my intelligent use of words

Should I be Miss Picasso and paint you a beautiful picture of verbal art

Should I be Miss Sensual and seduce your mind with tales of romantic encounters unknown

What kind of poet should I be?

Will they listen if I speak about current events and governmental conspiracy

Will they listen if I share my honest opinion about healthcare and why the focus should be on prevention

Will they listen if I reveal secrets about myself in coded metaphors

Will they listen if I speak about pain and hurt, poverty, and despair

Will they listen if I yell loudly and scream out my greatest fears

Will they listen

Maybe they will like me if I speak about hot summer days on the beach

Maybe they will like me if I tell them about that one time at band camp

Maybe they will like me if I remind them of the good ole days before bills and responsibility kicked in

Maybe they will like me if I pretend to be perfect and innocent

Maybe they will like me if I change my tone and mimic that of Shakespeare or Maya Angelou

Maybe they will like me

I can't put myself in a box deciding upon what type of poet Should I be

And who cares if they listen when I begin to speak my mind

Maybe they will like me, maybe they won't.

Either way, I'm not harmed

I can only be me.

I can get dressed, come out here, kick back and relax before a long week ahead

I can write my thoughts and share them on stage

I can be honest in the purity of my words and speak from my heart

I can focus on being true to myself and not worrying about What kind of poet should I be or will they listen and wondering if they will like me

I can only be me, and that has always been enough

Written by: Sharon V. Dickey 4/8/2014

"Am I ready to move forward or am I still too scared to come off the porch?" Sharon V. Dickey

Chapter 12

What Do You Want from Me?

Have you come closer to understanding who you are, realizing your worth, and learning to be comfortable and confident wearing those shoes? Before you can move forward into new things, you have to make sure you have dealt with your past and made peace with it so you can start fresh on a new path towards setting goals and fulfilling your destiny. You cannot continue to move forward from this point if you are still repeating the same behaviors. If you still ain't got it together, then reread the book up to this point again if you have to. If you are feeling confident and motivated and genuinely ready to do better and to be better, then let's keep it moving!

What is it that God wants you to do while you are here? That is a big question, right? And yes, I am bold enough to start out the gate with it. Let's get serious here. It's actually not as mysterious as it sounds. I won't say it is simple, but if you have your mind and spirit connected, this process to becoming the new you will be full of glorious testimonies! So, I ask again, what is it that God wants you to do while you are here? To answer that question, you must first find out what it is that you like. Sometimes, going to the negative and listing what you don't like feels easier. Today is a new day. It is a positivity-only day. When you begin to think about things you like, pay attention to how you feel in your body.

You may feel yourself smiling. You may notice your posture change to sitting up or standing straighter. Do you tilt your head to the side or start swinging your arms? Whatever cues to happiness that are present in your body are your unique way of saying to the world "this is what happy looks like on me." That happiness that is shining through is a result of you putting your best foot forward. Things that you really don't have to try that hard to do because they naturally are easy for you are your talents. Think about something you enjoy doing that you would not mind doing all day for free. It may seem small and insignificant to you, but it is huge in the lives of others. God gave you that talent specifically because he wants you to use it. My son has a natural ability to draw and paint. What do I buy him? Paint, paint brushes, canvases, and art classes. He is happy when he is drawing and painting. He is calm and at peace. He is focused and productive. He sold his first painting last year at 10 years old.

My daughter is lip gloss and nail polish all day. She creates her own accessories, and she loves shoes. One day she asked me for another pair of flips flops. I said, "no, I'm not buying you anymore flip flops." So, Miss MacGyver found a piece of cardboard and a rubber band. She took a pencil and traced her feet on the cardboard and cut it out. Then she somehow looped the rubber band between her toes and attached it to the cardboard. I really have no idea how she did it, but she made her own flip flops, and they were actually cute. So what do I buy her? Anything she wants out the arts and crafts department. She launched her jewelry making business two years ago. Those are examples of finding the things that come naturally to you and incorporating them into your life whether it is as a hobby for relaxation and stress management or for a business idea to create wealth for you and your family. Either way, God has said very clearly that his desire for us is to use our talents and He will Bless us for being obedient. Using your gifts is pleasing to God.

Proverbs 18:16 NKJV "A man's gift maketh room for him, and bringeth him before great men.".

Proverbs 10:22 NKJV "The blessing of the Lord makes one rich, and He adds no sorrow with it."

1 Timothy 4:14-16 NKJV "Do not neglect the gift that is in you, which was given to you by prophecy with the laying on of the hands of the eldership. 15 Meditate on these things; give yourself entirely to them, that your progress may be evident to all. 16 Take heed to yourself and to the doctrine. Continue in them, for in doing this you will save both yourself and those who hear you".

We spent a lot of time developing our self-awareness and improving our self-esteem. Now that you know who you are, it is time to decide where you are going and begin making a plan to get there. Start with finding your talent, and it will guide you the rest of the way. Some people have obvious talents like a beautiful voice, or you can play multiple instruments. And then you might be a master of many like me, where you can do a little bit of a lot of stuff, and that makes it a little more challenging to identify which one of these things you should be doing. Listening to other people can be good and bad, but sometimes people will see your talent or gift before you will. Consider the source when listening to people, but if many people are saying the exact same thing, then you should at least look into considering what they are suggesting as your possible gift and give it a try.

That is how I came to where I am today. I also discussed it with God. I literally ask Him, "God, what do you want me to do?". I was so tired of living outside of my purpose, so I begged God to show me clearly. I have been ready for years for the counseling portion of what I do. People have been sitting on my virtual couch for free for many years. I enjoy being a safe space for people to share what they are going through in their lives. I never give advice during my sessions and most of the time people have no idea they are even in a session. I merely guide them into finding their own understanding where they can make the best decision for themselves. I write books because I love to give advice and this is where I can say what I want and how I want and truly express myself. Counseling is therapy for you, writing books is therapy for me, and I truly love both of these things. I would consider them to be my passion along with my purpose. Take a look deep within, consort with Goad and ask yourself, what do you actually care about? What would you wake up and do for free every day? Would God consider that thing pleasing to Him? Lastly, are you uplifting the Kingdom by doing it?

"My goal is to actively work at being the best version of myself every day, and then improve upon that."

Sharon V. Dickey

Chapter 13

Keep Dreaming and Believing!

Setting goals, creating a plan of action, and working towards achieving those goals is not an easy task. Identifying your talent and tapping into what you believe is your purpose in life is probably the most challenging part of this journey you are own. I say challenging because when you truly know what your purpose it, it can sometimes be the scariest thing you could ever imagine doing. Often times, finding out what your purpose is and living in it requires you to take a leap of faith to achieve it. This leap is not a little hop across a crack in the sidewalk. This leap is literally run as fast as you can on a rooftop and once you reach the end, don't stop! Keep running! No, you don't know if the next building is close enough for you to land on. No, you don't know how high you are off the ground. All you know is there is nothing but open space and air all around you. There is no magical parachute that will appear out of nowhere to make your descent more comfortable. There is no inflatable rescue thingy below. All you have is your faith that if God gave you this purpose, then you will only need to depend on Him to keep you afloat. Based on what God has called you to do, your purpose may be expensive. God already knows the exact dollar amount you need to set your goal and create a workable plan of action to achieve your goal of living your purpose, and He will provide everything you need. You may have to make several goals to get to where you need to be on this journey, but that is okay too. God already knows this. Every step of the way in this process is purposeful and having faith and depending on Him is the only way you will make it. You can't get caught up worrying about the details. What I have learned is that you can't plan it all. I am a planner by nature, but once you decide to give it all to God, set your goal, and begin to work your way towards it, God will carry you the rest of the way. Don't worry about whether you will need a helmet or if you will have a window seat. Just buckle up, stay in prayer, and enjoy the ride. God's purpose and His plan for you are only for your good so hold on to that and let go. My grandmother would always say, "Jesus is my co-pilot," although I was clearly the one sitting in the passenger seat as she flew around those curbs in that little black Buick holding on for dear life. That's how I learned that prayer works. She increased my faith every time I got in the car with her or my grand aunt. What I love about her statement is yes, I am the one physically here in control of what I am doing, but at the same time, I have faith that God will still intervene on my behalf if I ever cut a corner too sharp or have to slam on breaks real fast because He already knows what is ahead of me. I don't have to worry because God got my back.

Living your purpose may seem impossible. Whatever God is calling you to do may seem completely unlike anything you would ever do. It may be something you enjoy that you never thought you would enhance the Kingdom by doing and definitely not providing for your family by doing, or it may be something that is going to push you completely out of your comfort zone where you will have to show the world all of that greatness you have been hiding. Either way, you are going to have to get up on that rooftop and just start running, in your head of course. There will be false starts, and you will get five strides in and be like, "you trippin' ". I ain't doing this!" and that is okay too because God already knew and factored in all the time you will spend procrastinating, and pre-planning, planning, and post-planning before you even make your first step. The anxiety you get when you even think about it may feel overwhelming. What you feel you are being asked to do may add up to be a negative impossible. What I can assure you of is if it is truly God's plan for your life, then as soon as you set your first goal and take that first step towards achieving your goal, everything will line up, and everything you need to make it happen will flow freely to you. You just have to expect it. Expect God to hold up his end of the bargain like He said He would and watch Him come through for you.

I remember when I was begging God to show me my purpose. It was like he was sitting there with His lips twisted and arms folded leaning back in a chair saying "really?" to me. I was like "yeah, really! Why you got an attitude with me?" Then He sucked his teeth and started shaking his head as I continued to throw my tantrum about not having any idea what He wanted me to do with my life. Then He gave me the silent treatment for the rest of the day. That night when I went to bed, I dreamed of people in my life who have all said the same thing to me which they repeated in my dream. "Sharon, you need to write a book. I always call you, and you never tell me what to do, but I always end up knowing exactly what I want to do after I finish talking to myself because you only said two words the whole time. You need to be some type of inspiring, motivational speaker. Girl, how you make this healthy food taste so good? You need to open a restaurant." Now, that wasn't one dream. That was several dreams with these reminders in them. I said, "God, I'll do what I can, but a few of these I can't get with. This is just too much, and it's all over the place. Imma need you to put them all together." Initially, I tried to attach them all in the way that other people gave it to me. Then after being burned out, I realized that I needed to see what exactly God wanted me to do with it. The only one I struggled with was cooking because it has never given me joy to be judged and I think my food is good, but who with a pot and a pan can't cook it themselves? All the others have been combined, and I genuinely believe I am honoring God with the work I am doing, and the best part is that I get to be me--100% just me. I enjoy being free to be me. I enjoy helping others. I enjoy being of service. He has provided multiple ways for me to be a blessing through spoken and written words. I was hoping the cooking would fade into the background and be one that I just leave on the table, but it bothered me that I know God gave it to me, but I had not been able to successfully figure out what He wanted me to do with it. Actually, I do know, and I know it will come back around, and I know exactly how it will come back around, but for now, He has provided a way for me to share some of it with you, but not through me so I can remain comfortable for now. I don't know about you, but sometimes I feel like God has set me up.

When my twins turned one it finally hit me that I was somebody's mama, I thanked God for thinking so highly of me that He put me of all people in charge of two people at one time. Then I started thinking, ummm, if He thinks I can handle this, what else is He about to throw on me? The set up was real, and I thank Him for trusting me to be who He knew I would become. It was not easy getting here, and I have a very long way to go. My journey is not over because I'm writing this second book. This is the very beginning of a long road ahead. I am just getting started, and every day, I am finding myself amid the process.

Setting goals, daily, weekly, monthly, and yearly will keep you focused on fulfilling your purpose and staying on the right path on your journey. If you have no idea where to start with creating a goal, then your first step will be to find something that needs to be done. Whether it is self-improvement or improving your community, if it is in line with your purpose, which will be something that will be pleasing to God and enhance the Kingdom, then set a date. Determine what you need to get it done, ask God to send the people to help you and have faith that it will all work out fine. I have a friend who enjoys cutting grass. He now owns his own landscaping business, but he started out mowing yards on the side. His work is pleasing to God, and it enhances the Kingdom because every person he meets gets to know Jesus a little better because of their encounter with him. I have another friend who enjoys cutting hair. He and his wife own their own barber and beauty salon. Their work is pleasing to God, and everyone whom they encounter draws closer to God because of their time spent in their chairs. I know of this guy who has a great personality, and he is absolutely hilarious. He openly shares his story of how he became a Gospel comedian and now tells jokes for the Lord. They all had a spark of inspiration and a passion for something they enjoyed doing, that led them to set their goals, create a workable plan of action, and step out on faith to fulfilling their dreams and living in their purpose.

As you get your notebook and pen and sit down to write out your goal, first write your purpose at the top of the page. Then list three ways that your purpose will be pleasing to God and enhance the Kingdom. Write down how others will have an opportunity to see God in you by fulfilling this purpose. Then write three short term goals. The first one is something very small and easily achievable like making the necessary phone calls to check an available date, or schedule to call someone and ask them to be your mentor. Set the completion date for one week from the current day. The next goal should require a little more work, and it may be something you have to schedule in advance. Make that goal end date one month from the current date. Once you have met that goal, set another goal with a 30-day end date as well and keep setting monthly goals that will build upon each other, so you continue to make progress towards your purpose. The third goal should begin to push you out of your comfort zone. This goal should be big. Your monthly goals should be setting you up to achieve this really huge goal which will have an end date one year from the current date. That's the game changer goal. Don't be scared to set this one. You have a whole year to achieve it. That year will fly by really fast, but you will be prepared for it because you are working your plan towards your purpose every month. Stay encouraged and stay inspired knowing that what you are working on is something you will enjoy once you get up the courage to just do it. You've spent enough time daydreaming about it and fantasizing about how great your life will be if you could just do it. Now you can do it! You have finally reached that point in your life where it is time to be about it! Go live and be free and do what God is calling you to do!

"God spoke, but I've been too scared to obey. Not anymore though. I conquered no worry, now I'm conquering no fear!!" Sharon V. Dickey

Chapter 14

No Worry, No Fear

Those are the words I spoke in response to my brother saying he was proud of me the night I launched my website www.sharondickey.com. It was a fantastic feeling to know that your family is happy for your success and supports you through your journey. However, you may find that there are times where nobody has your back. Do not expect people to give you what they do not know how to give. You may have just crossed a milestone in your life where you have accomplished something incredible. Let's just say between the last chapter and this one, you took some time to figure out your purpose and you are ready to walk in it! You're excited! You're smiling from ear-to-ear! You can't wait to share this important stage in your life with your loved ones, so you begin to tell people. This is where we need to back up a second and think this thing through. You have the desire to share a special moment in your life, and the first people you may think of are your spouse, significant other, parents, the rest of your immediate family and your closest friends. Just because a person is worthy of the close family or friend title doesn't mean they will share your excitement about your accomplishments. What is important is for you to identify who is in your fan club and who is not. The last thing you need is your Eeyore (the character from Winnie the Pooh, for all of you 80's babies) acting and sounding cousin you grew up with like sisters to place a grey cloud over your sunshiny day. Make a mental note of who displays the qualities of your fan club members. Envision yourself as the big star you truly are, and that millions of people love and adore you for being. No matter where you go, you're always met with people crowding around you and cheering you on. They send you letters every month telling you how completely awesome you are, and no matter what you are doing, big or small, it doesn't matter, they always support you and give you the energy you need to keep pushing forward. I have close family and friends that I call my fan club. I count on them to keep expecting greatness from me so I can reach these goals I set every year. "Everything I do, I do for my fans", that's what I say as I stand on stage amongst millions of people yelling my name and wearing pictures of me on their t-shirts. Well, actually I'm just in my car driving down the street on my way to the grocery store in my lounge clothes, but in my mind, I'm making star status moves.

Who is in your fan club? You just got a promotion on your job. Who do you tell first? Vetting your fan club members is uber important. If you call someone and say, "Hey you know how I hated my job, right? But I held on and waited for God to move, and I got hired for this better job today!" Those first five people you tell should be the executive officers of your fan club.

Have you ever been in a situation where you have shared some good news with someone who's usually very nice to you, only to get crickets? You know good and well they got your text. They respond to every text you send except for this one. What's different in the way your conversations have been going. Have you been more of the backseat person while they have been shining out front? That would be a sign of jealousy, pay attention to that. Are you normally the one needing advice and they usually are successful at giving you advice and helping to solve your issues? That is a sign of a person who needs to feel important. What if they are a special friend, potential boo-thang-type friend approaching 90 days? You tell them about something exciting in your life, and they don't say a word to you for a whole 24 hours, and then when they do its void of enthusiasm and lacks real concern or support of your future. That's definitely not the type of new love interest I want in my life.

What I find to be true is when people are not happy with themselves, they cannot be happy for you. Don't expect someone to act like a fan club member when they don't have a fan club themselves. When you celebrate others, you are confirming to God that He is real, and you can see Him moving in people's lives. This opens up the door for you to receive your blessings. Unfortunately, people who don't have their stuff together, don't know how to be supportive and a source of encouragement for people who do. This is where you may find you have to leave some people behind. Your family members and friends may not be able to tag along with you into this next stage of your life. Cutting people off and focusing on your purpose can sometimes feel lonely and you may want to turn back to those people who were not pushing you forward. This is where the devil is trying to get slick because he sees you headed up the mountain to your destiny and this is his last chance to knock you off the cliff. Don't let the devil use other people to defeat you. Stay focused no matter what is thrown at you. Not having the support of the people closest to you is hurtful and it can make you feel like you are too high up and need to come back down to where they are. Never diminish yourself to increase someone else. What I mean is never feel obligated to shine less to make other people comfortable being around you. They are not experiencing the real you, and at some point, you are going to burst out and shine ever so brightly, then you'll see they have always been a grey cloud. It is ok to want those around you to find their sunshine so they can bling in the sky along with you, but that is their journey to finding themselves by finding God. Your journey requires you to stay on your own path. That place where God wants you to go is tailor-made for you, and it simply is not big enough to carry everybody with you. Those people hanging on your back and attached to your hip have to be dropped off because you can't get through the door with them holding you down. Sometimes these people aren't revealed until the very end, but if you look back on your life, you'll see how they were right there holding you back the whole time. It's time for you to break free!

This last hike up the mountain to your destiny is yours to go alone leaving behind all the toxic people you chose to allow into your life. Get ready to receive your new friend requests. Remember, He has your best interest at heart, and He is the only one you can indeed count on. Now, the job

He has for you to do, you may need some help, but once you pray and ask God for his Angels, He will send His people to surround you. These people may not look like you. These people may be from a completely different background than you. Understand He is placing you amongst the people that you are transforming into. You are entering into a group of like-minded individuals, and at first, it will seem like a foreign land, like you don't speak the language or understand the culture, but you will see in each person the light that shines in you. You all will connect on familiar accords, and if you work together and build new friendships and alliances, the access to the power you have collectively will keep you moving forward and accomplishing every goal you set.

At this point, you know who you are, you have decided where you want to go, and now God is going to send the resources to get you there. You have to trust the process and enjoy the highs and the lows of the journey. You will begin to notice how every encounter is purposeful to your success in life. Keep pushing forward! You've come too far to turn back now! You've done the work. You have dealt with your past. You have cut people off. You have set your short-term and long-term goals. You have mapped out a workable plan for your future. Most importantly, you have discovered that there is no value high enough for Your Price of Admission because you are priceless! You are fearfully and wonderfully made, and there is no dollar amount you can place on God's greatness. Now is the time to walk boldly in the presence of the Lord with No worries and No Fear!

Peace & Blessings!
Sharon V. Dickey

www.ingramcontent.com/pod-product-compliance
Lightning Source LLC
Chambersburg PA
CBHW050644160426
43194CB00010B/1804